You
are my
Sunshine

summersdale

An Hachette UK Company
www.hachette.co.uk

Summersdale Publishers
Part of Octopus Publishing Group Limited
Carmelite House
50 Victoria Embankment
LONDON
EC4Y 0DZ
UK

www.summersdale.com

This FSC® label means
that materials used for
the product have been
responsibly sourced

MIX
Paper | Supporting
responsible forestry
FSC® C016973

The authorized representative in the EEA is Hachette Ireland,
8 Castlecourt Centre, Dublin 15, D15 XTP3, Ireland (email: info@hbgi.ie)

Printed and bound in China

ISBN: 978-1-83799-660-5

Substantial discounts on bulk quantities of Summersdale books
are available to corporations, professional associations and other
organizations. For details contact general enquiries: telephone:
+44 (0) 1243 771107 or email: enquiries@summersdale.com.

To..

From..

Many people will walk in and out of your life, but only true friends will leave footprints in your heart.

Eleanor Roosevelt

Shared joy is a
double joy; shared
sorrow is half
a sorrow.

Swedish proverb

You make the greyest of days brighter

"STAY"
IS A
CHARMING
WORD IN
A FRIEND'S
VOCABULARY.

Amos Bronson Alcott

Each friend represents a world in us, a world possibly not born until they arrive.

Anaïs Nin

A good friend is…
a tie to the past,
a road to the
future, the key
to sanity.

Lois Wyse

Thank you for being you

Friendship... flourishes not so much by kindnesses as by sincerity.

Étienne de La Boétie

A friend is someone who knows all about you and still loves you.

Elbert Hubbard

FRIENDSHIP IS THE GREATEST THERAPY

What you want is someone who will take the bus with you when the limo breaks down.

Oprah Winfrey

Against the assault of laughter, nothing can stand.

Mark Twain

Friends are true twins in soul.

William Penn

I CHERISH EVERYTHING ABOUT YOU

Those who bring sunshine into the lives of others cannot keep it from themselves.

J. M. Barrie

From the spirit's choice and free desire, needing no oath of legal bond, is friend bestowed on friend.

Dietrich Bonhoeffer

You give me reasons to smile

Friendship's the wine of life.

Edward Young

Two things you will never have to chase: true friends and true love.

Mandy Hale

I always felt that the great high privilege, relief and comfort of friendship, was that one had to explain nothing.

Katherine Mansfield

YOU BRING
OUT MY
BEST SELF

True friendship is like sound health; the value of it is seldom known until it be lost.

Charles Caleb Colton

Friends are like melons. Shall I tell you why? To find one good, you must a hundred try.

Claude Mermet

You lift me
up when
I'm down

A real friend is one who walks in when the rest of the world walks out.

Anonymous

Friends are the
sunshine of life.

John Hay

Friends accept you the way you are.

Marilyn Monroe

YOU ALWAYS
REASSURE ME

I am wealthy in my friends.

William Shakespeare

When we give
cheerfully and
accept gratefully,
everyone is blessed.

Maya Angelou

You know me
better than I
know myself

SOME SOULS JUST UNDERSTAND EACH OTHER UPON MEETING.

N. R. Hart

I will follow you
to the ends of
the world.

Khaled Hosseini

The better part of
one's life consists
of his friendships.

Abraham Lincoln

YOU BELIEVE
IN ME

A friend is someone whose face you can see in the dark.

Frances O'Roark Dowell

The friend who
holds your hand
and says the wrong
thing is made of
dearer stuff than
the one who
stays away.

Barbara Kingsolver

FRIENDS LIKE YOU ARE PRECIOUS

An unshared happiness is not happiness.

Boris Pasternak

One joy scatters
a hundred griefs.

Chinese proverb

Some people go to priests; others to poetry; I to my friends.

Virginia Woolf

You have
my back

For a friend with an understanding heart is worth no less than a brother.

Homer

If you have nothing in life but a good friend, you're rich.

Michelle Kwan

You're always honest

NO MAN IS USELESS WHILE HE HAS A FRIEND.

Robert Louis Stevenson

Find a group
of people who
challenge and
inspire you; spend
a lot of time with
them, and it will
change your life.

Amy Poehler

There is no investment you can make which will pay you so well as the effort to scatter sunshine and good cheer.

Orison Swett Marden

Thank you for all that you've taught me

Laughter is a sunbeam of the soul.

Thomas Mann

Wherever you go, no matter what the weather, always bring your own sunshine.

Anthony J. D'Angelo

I'M LUCKY
TO HAVE
YOU

The most beautiful discovery true friends make is that they can grow separately without growing apart.

Elisabeth Foley

In the sweetness of friendship let there be laughter and sharing of pleasures.

Kahlil Gibran

Only your real friends will tell you when your face is dirty.

Sicilian proverb

You always
know how to
cheer me up

Of all things granted us by wisdom, none is greater or better than friendship.

Pietro Aretino

A best friend
is like a four-
leaf clover:
hard to find and
lucky to have.

Sarah Jessica Parker

A friend is someone who gives you total freedom to be yourself – and especially to feel, or not feel.

Jim Morrison

If you live your
life with kindness
and give other
people great energy,
that beauty and
great energy come
back to you.

Beyoncé

YOU ARE ALWAYS IN MY HEART

Few delights can equal the mere presence of one whom we trust utterly.

George MacDonald

Let us learn
to show our
friendship for
a man when he
is alive and not
after he is dead.

F. Scott Fitzgerald

YOU INSPIRE ME

When it comes to friends, it's not how much time you spend with them, just how you spend it!

Eiichiro Oda

Friendship isn't a big thing – it's a million little things.

Anonymous

My friends are my estate.

Emily Dickinson

YOU HAVE
A HEART
OF GOLD

Friends are those rare people who ask how we are and then wait to hear the answer.

Ed Cunningham

If you haven't learned the meaning of friendship, you really haven't learned anything.

Muhammad Ali

We always have fun together

WHAT DO YOU MOST VALUE IN YOUR FRIENDS? THEIR CONTINUED EXISTENCE.

Christopher Hitchens

Care about the beings you care about in gorgeous and surprising ways.

Anne Herbert

No love, no friendship, can cross the path of our destiny without leaving some mark on it forever.

François Mauriac

You help me
to see my
strengths

The ornament of a house is the friends who frequent it.

Ralph Waldo Emerson

To love and be loved is the greatest happiness of existence.

Sydney Smith

I KNOW
THAT I CAN
ALWAYS
TURN TO
YOU

I can trust my friends. These people force me to examine myself and encourage me to grow.

Cher

A true friend never gets in your way unless you happen to be going down.

Arnold H. Glasow

If I am not touching a life, I am not touching life.

Craig D. Lounsbrough

YOU GIVE
THE BEST
ADVICE

I don't know what I would have done so many times in my life if I hadn't had my girlfriends.

Reese Witherspoon

We must ever be
friends; and of
all who offer you
friendship let
me be ever the
first, the truest,
the nearest and
dearest!

Henry Wadsworth Longfellow

You're the
light at the
end of the
tunnel

The universe only makes sense when we have someone to share our feelings with.

Paulo Coelho

Sometimes people are beautiful. Not in looks. Not in what they say. Just in what they are.

Markus Zusak

THERE'S NOTHING LIKE A REALLY LOYAL, DEPENDABLE, GOOD FRIEND.

Jennifer Aniston

I CAN'T BE
SAD WHEN
YOU'RE
AROUND

Love is rarer than genius itself. And friendship is rarer than love.

Charles Péguy

A true friend is one who overlooks your failures and tolerates your success!

Doug Larson

LIFE IS
BETTER
WITH YOU

A real friendship should not fade as time passes, and should not weaken because of space separation.

John Newton

I would rather walk with a friend in the dark, than alone in the light.

Helen Keller

The finest friendships are between those who can do without each other.

Elbert Hubbard

You listen
when I
need help

There is nothing I would not do for those who are really my friends. I have no notion of loving people by halves.

Jane Austen

A good companion
shortens the
longest road.

Kurdish proverb

You know
how to make
me laugh

THE BEST WAY TO CHEER YOURSELF UP IS TO TRY TO CHEER SOMEBODY ELSE UP.

Mark Twain

Rare as is true love, true friendship is rarer.

Jean de La Fontaine

One friend with
whom you have a lot
in common is better
than three with
whom you struggle
to find things to
talk about.

Mindy Kaling

YOU TURN
SADNESS
INTO JOY

Fate chooses our relatives; we choose our friends.

Jacques Delille

True friendship resists time, distance and silence.

Isabel Allende

You always
encourage
me to keep
trying

Some friendships are made by nature, some by contract, some by interest, and some by souls.

Jeremy Taylor

If you have one true friend, you have more than your share.

Thomas Fuller

True friends are like diamonds – bright, beautiful, valuable, and always in style.

Nicole Richie

YOU LIFT
MY SPIRITS

Words are easy, like the wind; faithful friends are hard to find.

Richard Barnfield

THERE IS NOTHING BETTER THAN A FRIEND, UNLESS IT IS A FRIEND WITH CHOCOLATE.

Linda Grayson

A day spent
with you is a
day well spent

The greatest
gift of life is
friendship, and I
have received it.

Hubert Humphrey

The truth is: everyone is going to hurt you. You just got to find the ones worth suffering for.

Bob Marley

All who joy would win must share it. Happiness was born a twin.

Lord Byron

YOU FILL
MY LIFE
WITH FUN

I think about my best friendship... as like a great romance of my young life.

Lena Dunham

Friendship is always a sweet responsibility, never an opportunity.

Kahlil Gibran

YOU ALWAYS KNOW THE RIGHT THING TO SAY

Friendship is a sheltering tree.

Samuel Taylor Coleridge

A friend's eye is a good mirror.

Irish proverb

The only way we can get by in this world is through the help we receive from others.

Amy Poehler

THANK YOU
FOR BEING
THERE
FOR ME

Sometimes the most ordinary things could be made extraordinary, simply by doing them with the right people.

Nicholas Sparks

You can't deny laughter; when it comes, it plops down in your favourite chair and stays as long as it wants.

Stephen King

You take
pride in my
achievements

I FEEL THAT THERE IS NOTHING MORE TRULY ARTISTIC THAN TO LOVE PEOPLE.

Vincent van Gogh

There is no exercise better for the heart than reaching down and lifting people up.

John Andrew Holmes

Let us be grateful
to the people who
make us happy –
they are the
charming gardeners
who make our
souls blossom.

Marcel Proust

YOUR ZEST
FOR LIFE IS
CONTAGIOUS

True happiness arises... from the friendship and conversation of a few select companions.

Joseph Addison

The kindest way of helping yourself is to find a friend.

Ann Kaiser Stearns

You remind me that I am loved

Growing apart doesn't change the fact that for a long time we grew side by side; our roots will always be tangled.

Ally Condie

The jewel in my dower, I would not wish any companion in the world but you.

William Shakespeare

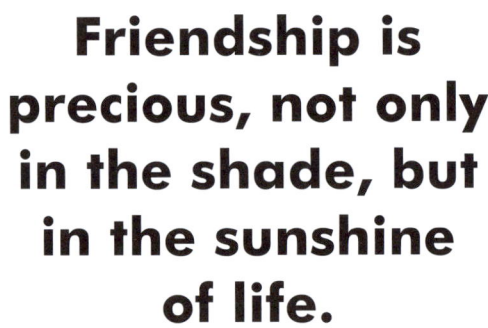

Friendship is precious, not only in the shade, but in the sunshine of life.

Thomas Jefferson

Nothing changes when we've been apart

BEST FRIEND, MY WELL-SPRING IN THE WILDERNESS!

George Eliot

No one is useless
in this world
who lightens the
burdens of another.

Charles Dickens

I VALUE
YOUR
KINDNESS
AND
HONESTY

There is one
friend in the life
of each of us
who seems not a
separate person...
but an expansion,
an interpretation,
of one's self.

Edith Wharton

Good friends help you find important things when you have lost them... your smile, your hope, and your courage.

Doe Zantamata

Life is an awful, ugly place to not have a best friend.

Sarah Dessen

YOU'RE MY
ANCHOR

We have each of
us cause to think
with deep gratitude
of those who have
lighted the flames
within us.

Albert Schweitzer

A friend is a person with whom I may be sincere. Before him I may think aloud.

Ralph Waldo Emerson

Since there is nothing so well worth having as friends, never lose a chance to make them.

Francesco Guicciardini

I can
always
depend
on you

For friendship makes prosperity more shining and lessens adversity by dividing and sharing it.

Cicero

A friend may be waiting behind a stranger's face.

Maya Angelou

Friendship is the greatest of worldly goods. Certainly, to me it is the chief happiness of life.

C. S. Lewis

I felt it shelter to speak to you.

Emily Dickinson

YOU ARE MY
SUNSHINE

Have you enjoyed this book?
If so, find us on Facebook at
Summersdale Publishers, on
Twitter/X at **@Summersdale** and
on Instagram and TikTok at
@summersdalebooks and get in
touch. We'd love to hear from you!

www.summersdale.com